THE ITALIAN GARDEN

HARRY N. ABRAMS, INC., PUBLISHERS, NEW YORK

THE ITALIAN GARDEN

PHOTOGRAPHS BY GEOFFREY JAMES

ESSAY BY ROBERT HARBISON

This book is for my mother,
a small token in return for everything she did for us.
G.J.

===

Editor: Ruth A. Peltason

Designer: Carol A. Robson

Page 1: Villa Medici. Niobe and Her Children
Page 3: Villa Chigi. The Villa from the Main Axis
Page 26: Villa Lante. Fountain at Entrance with Giambologna's Pegasus

Library of Congress Cataloging-in-Publication Data

James, Geoffrey, 1942–
The Italian garden/photographs by Geoffrey James; essay by Robert Harbison.
128 p.   cm.
ISBN 0-8109-3456-6
1. Gardens, Italian — Italy.   2. Gardens, Italian — Italy — Pictorial
works.   I. Harbison, Robert.   II. Title.
SB457.85.J36   1991
712'.6'0945 — dc20   90-45915
CIP

Published in 1991 by Harry N. Abrams, Incorporated, New York
A Times Mirror Company

Printed and bound in Japan

CONTENTS

Essay by Robert Harbison 6

The Gardens 26

VILLA CHIGI, CETINALE

THE VILLA FROM THE WALK

THE ITALIAN GARDEN
BY
ROBERT HARBISON

With careful planning, you could come to certain Italian gardens along fairly rustic lanes. The object of the exercise is to smooth the transition between the garden and the world outside. You don't want to pop into it straight from the motorway or the traffic jam you find nowadays in Frascati. But why not? Don't gardens *exist* to provide such escapes, and isn't Hadrian's Villa an even more soothing experience because the approach to Tivoli is now so hideous? Who can any longer imagine Fragonard straying over its desecrated slopes?

The gardens of Italy become idealized when filtered by memory or eighteenth-century French painters. They are like buildings which have collapsed and then turned to leafage, soft and incomplete remains of an imposing civilization. Their wild beasts are petrified and covered with moss, their owners long since fled. The last event which took place in them happened long ago. Time, after gaining ascendancy, ground to a halt.

They aren't gardens at all in the prosaic sense of the word. As the purpose of bits of masonry has become obscure, so the identity of plant species is now lost, and they have ceased to flower because no one demands it. Perhaps not just human neglect but biological torpor is levelling all those distinctions, and the species are reverting to an amorphous, primordial *green.* They aren't ilex, cypress, box, but just shade in general, no friend to light.

The paths are regular but occasionally blocked, by fallen trees or abandoned tools. They aren't long, but they are desolate, like any record of planning now forgotten. There are no birds, gardeners, or visitors; an entranced silence reigns.

Such is the Italian garden one constructs from far away. In reality, the absence of birds is the work of hungry cats who circulate in the underbrush, and the neglect which we count their main charm is a civilized contrivance. It hurts to give up one's dream of Italy (based, probably, in the eighteenth century), but there are compensations.

Yet, as one keeps retreating from a too-glaring sun, one goes back on the promise to see Italian gardens *as they really are.* It's an art-form (hideous word) which tolerates and breeds illusions. They inhere in the names for an Italian garden's parts: *giardino segreto* — how many times will you hear that before you accept that it doesn't mean a mystery, that the plot it refers to isn't hidden or hard to find? True, it is usually small, sunken, and intense, but it may lie right below the house.

There is one famous Italian garden I don't like, maybe because of what it has become, the Doria Pamphily in Rome. Now it is a public park, and well trampled over; it couldn't keep a secret, though doubtless you could still get lost there. After a long and pointless introduction (you can't enter by the villa's original gate but must traverse irrelevant parcels of land acquired by later owners) you reach its famous *giardino segreto,* one of the largest in existence, a platform of furled-up box parterres with a scattering of dried-up fountains. As often happens in state-run gardens, this intensely planted bit is closed to the public. That's how it is secret: clearly visible, but unenterable. So you gnash your teeth at its gates and climb to see it from above, or circle the fence until the view is blocked by the house, a seventeenth-century building which looks like a nineteenth.

Maybe segreto really means *closed.* Certainly Italians have no appetite for the concealment practiced in English gardens like Hidcote. In Italian ones, you can usually see every part at once, at the point of entry, though a first-time visitor has no way of knowing this. Not that they don't contain surprises — many defunct, of course: the famous water jokes no longer work, wetting your face or clothes as you stop at a statue or lean on a railing — but these don't consist of whole new worlds you stumble into. English gardens enjoy confusing you about their plan. Hidcote is relentlessly formal in its parts and very jumbled overall. One of the delights there is the non-communicating nature of the whole.

You can almost hear an Italian visitor crying 'foul play.' Italian gardens are always more frank about their purposes. Not without horrible breaches of decorum no English garden would stomach, but you always know where you are.

VILLA RIZZARDI, NEAR VERONA

BOSCO

The most touching sign of the Italian lack of interest in misleading the visitor or deforming his sense of where he is, is that amazing institution, the *bosco*. Every garden has one. The practiced visitor checks as he enters to fix its location, size, and stance toward the whole. The largest bosco isn't large. Sometimes you cannot see across them, but you can always walk their greatest dimension in a couple of minutes. I don't know if it's safe to say Italians don't *like* large gardens, but you can say that it isn't really how they *imagine* them. There are plenty of exceptions, Marlia, Caserta, and others, but they spring from the eighteenth century and later. Maybe they got that way under French or English influence, because the greatest *Italian* contributions to the art are always formidably compact.

So the true bosco isn't a place you could get lost in. Often there are the most comfortable views from its borders, which will be banked up above the surrounding fields, on which you look down as from a toy domain. Even the wood is like a little town standing out against the landscape.

Sometimes, as at Gamberaia, the bosco is no more than a green closet which barely surrounds you, but it is enough. Its real use is to provide a retreat from the sun, enough shade to cover one person. It's an extra dividend if you get a fleeting hint of the tree-covered world which preceded civilization. And it is somehow a piece of Italian realism that you can never cut loose in this fantasy (as you can in English parks); that stage of history remains a distant memory. So the wood isn't a wild wood. It always has its stone table and chairs, and grants an artificial distance from life in the house which is not even out of earshot. Yet I came under a powerful illusion at one of the simplest of these fabrications.

The Corsi Salviati in Sesto Fiorentino has no business to be as wonderful as it is. A truly hideous street, a long bleak building which you pass through like a wall, and then you are in a large garden-room of great and artless charm.

The secret of Italy is lurking here, pompous yet supremely nonchalant; rich, haphazard, and founded on such deep reservoirs of life in society that one will never plumb them. There's a profound historical reason why such a

LA GAMBERAIA, SETTIGNANO

THE MAIN AXIS

garden feels free to strike off in one direction after another, as if ideas flew past very rapidly and lasted about a minute each. One axis is established and then another; there are several centers, of equal weight and slightly different size; it promulgates different, unmatched symmetries.

Around it runs a glorious wall, from which Henry James could extract the whole meaning of civilization, a gorgeous backdrop which creates an effective prison, a brocade blinding one to what lies beyond, except that it is breached by a senseless number of gates, as if the goal is to divide the length equally between solid and pierced. The view through every one of these gates is the same, for outside the wall lies an olive grove, whose trees always line up to form an alley which in most cases is only notional.

This wall is like a hastily strung masonry curtain, its swoops like the sagging of cloth. Turning the other way, we see the house doing the same thing—prolonging itself beyond its real extent for the sake of symmetry or pomp with thin and roofless tissue through whose windows we glimpse the sky. Along its top, a frill of railing, and wall-less pavilions. The whole is a theater set, which turns smaller stagelets toward the garden, in the form of grottoes with painted birds and an aviary with none.

So the garden feels itself at the center, not the edge, of this world. To a sober visitor from abroad its rules sound frivolous in the extreme. Larger plants are only permitted around the perimeter; in the center nothing must upstage the statues. Of these there is a truly hilarious profusion. If you stop to count them, the result is surprising—there are only twelve. The rest of the chattering crowd is made up by lemon trees in pots, whose heights are the same as the figures' and whose different shapes break the monotony without changing the consistency.

In Italian gardens you are never alone, not that they are heavily visited: outside the summer months you'll usually have them to yourself. But they are populated before you arrive by these stone gesturers. Italian statues don't stand still like English ones, but engage in discourse, not with each other particularly, though the presence of the others keeps them from looking demented the way the single charging or orating figures on American memorials tend to do.

And this profusion accounts for a corresponding bleakness in the planting. To foreign eyes, at first, the proportions are all wrong. There is so much stone to so little leaf, so much sun-baked masonry and gravel, that at midday it's more like a desert than a garden. But this is the intellectual rigor or the horticultural prudence of Italian parterres. In those conditions one wants to give as few hostages as possible to the watering can or the hose. So the proportions may not be so different from the average weed-grown façade — a lot of crumbling stone and a sprinkling of dusty vegetation.

But back, finally, to the bosco at Corsi Salviati: the parterre is a miracle, from which the bosco is a relief. As I remember, it narrows to a point as it gets farthest from the house. In the absence of a plan I can't check this: I'm only uneasy because that's how you *tend* to remember these places — steadily increasing seclusion like some trick of perspective. Here I imagined a Lampedusa figure, bent over from the happy, heavy weight of tradition, coming often, not to write his memoirs, but to construct a freer life with some chosen companion, a woman of his own age.

Different *boschi* fuse together or get mistaken for each other; it's the really anonymous parts of gardens. I'm troubled by a fear that the Lampedusa bosco is actually appended to a different garden on the other side of Italy, the Buonaccorsi south of Ancona. But after all, that's the region to which the Virgin Mary's hut flew through the air from Nazareth, coming to rest on a wooded hillside at Loreto and attracting a fancy marble casing, a large Gothic church on top of that, and so on, a supreme instance of civilization paying its obliterating respects to rudeness. So if one's imagination is inclined to transport and rearrange the features of one's favorite gardens, the vicinity of Loreto might give a sort of warrant for it.

Did you dream it, or did it happen? Is there really such a place as the Buonaccorsi, populated by overdressed queens wielding scepters, rustic beaus raising stone flowers to their noses, old men bearing cornucopias like torches? A place where religious emotions shade into clumsy jokes, where the chapel hides behind a mask of yew, and swooning saints look on at the antics of a clockwork devil. By some queer twist the stately Roman emperors are a little smaller than the dwarves who thrust out their lanterns and feel their way in full sun, or hoist their string of dead pheasants, or pull their giant daggers.

It sounds ridiculous. And even more beautiful parts sound more ridiculous still. At the center of the grotto is a languid shepherd-huntsman of painted wood who raises a battered horn to his lips. Behind him, a Turk and a harlequin, and between them a niche which contains tiny blacksmiths laboring at an anvil.

Formerly all these figures would have come alive as you approached, in a miniature pounding, tinkling, and tooting. The statues in this garden remind you of Tiepolo, the toys of Mozart. It is a gently spiritual place which lures you away from disbelief, until clowns are not grotesque but purveyors of a kind of music which has been detected running through all the forms of the world.

In its spiritual ambitions this seems a bit of high terrain. Spatially it is modest, the most inconspicuous version of a garden on a slope. It divides the hillside into five or six terraces like an ample flight of stairs. From above or below the sight of all those bobbing heads — the statues one hasn't met yet, or is returning to meet again — fills one with sociable anticipation.

Walking along the most beautiful and full of these little streets is like conversation, interspersed with delicate pattern: beds edged in stone make pentagons or many pointed stars. The path is punctuated, too, by obelisks halfway brought to life, poised on little feet and sprouting a face on each facet, which in turn spits out a length of cloth from which dangle fruit and flowers.

Experts say this is an eighteenth-century garden, but its origins are undocumented. Whenever they were actually carved, the obelisks are a survival of authentically Mannerist feeling. Stuck where it is, imperceptibly enlarged over the centuries, this garden is a shining example of the way outdoor harmonies defeat the historian. Old pictures of such places are fascinating (a gorgeous one survives at Buonaccorsi), and we welcome any amount of detail about restorations (that immemorial place, the Corsi Salviati, is a sympathetic resurrection of 1907), and yet . . . gardens which really work their spells elude such understanding. Then they aren't composites or palimpsests any more, but enchantments which it is rude to query.

VILLA CHIGI, CETINALE

THE VILLA GARDEN

There are exceptions to this censorious rule. The greatest of all Italian gardens is the greatest exception. Not that even the Villa Lante embodies a single conception or dates from a single time only. But unlike most of the others it exhibits throughout signs of the fusing intelligence which makes a great work of art. Lante reminds us how rare is a garden coherent like a great building. Gardening doesn't take the same skills as architecture; one can't transfer to or diffuse over the larger terrain identical principles. But Villa Lante is transformed by architectural intelligence met in this sustained way nowhere else.

Still, it is no textbook where lessons have shouldered aside the odor of the earth and the color of the light. Vignola, if it was he, has made his building of shadow and murmur, of the hill and the stream, of the way certain orders are lost and found again as they thread their way through the subsisting soil.

Villa Lante, like all the most famous and characteristic Italian gardens, is built on a steep incline, a fact which is a delight and a torment, a source of complexity and trouble, of unnatural change and welcome surprise. The hill is always there, perhaps more as rival than friend, to be watched closely, uncertain what it will do next. And then there is the water, lifeblood of the garden, most precious perhaps when reduced to the thinnest trickle, or when allowed to go underground for a moment so we wait for its reappearance. Coming down the slope at Bagnaia, it goes through many changes, racing on the water stair, almost stopping when it reaches the long dining table (where it purls down the center to cool the wine), finally ending in a spectacular fountain where four athletic Moors hold up a little mountain (the family crest) which gets sprayed, like the larger hill behind, by the declining stream.

This fountain is a later embellishment, and this crest was foreign to the garden's first deviser, Cardinal Gambara, whose own badge, the crayfish or *gambero*, presides at both ends of the water stair in monstrous enlargement.

Lante is more carefully orchestrated than its rivals and has therefore provoked comprehensive, if arcane, interpretation. Roughly speaking, it is thought to embody the history of the world moving from savagery to civilization. The large park outside the inner wall, which began as a hunting preserve, is now hard to recognize as the Silver Age before cities, denuded as it is of the statues and fountains which would alert one to this.

Otherwise, to follow the historical ages you must reverse the natural order of a visit. In the scheme, time runs downhill, but all visitors begin by ascending. At the top they see the break in human history which the Deluge is and the consequent starting-over, represented by the grotto, and they re-descend, progressively tamer, until they come to buildings and flat ground, or full-fledged civilization, and nothing higher than low hedges of four different heights.

Some people like mental schemes more than others, and I can't be sure Cardinal Gambara didn't, but this scenario takes no account of some of the garden's most delightful features, like the diagonal walks cut through a last steep incline covered in hedge, before the plain. Why has no one ever thought of this before, one of the primal geometric encounters, in which you understand a pyramid by acting it out?

As their lack of interest in plants may be forced on them by their climate, so the Italian predilection for slopes may be dictated by terrain. Or have they in the first place chosen an impregnable spot for a villa, as though it were a fort, and then needed to make the best of the attendant circumstances?

I am baffled by Italian attitudes to landscape. Certainly there's no such reverence for it as is widespread in England. One ideal, which you find in Renaissance paintings, is a range of toy hills, each with something built on top of it, like a cherry on an ice cream sundae. But sometimes I think the idea of landscape has barely entered Italian consciousness. Because they'd never expect a whole countryside to form itself into anything, they just don't look at it as a whole.

It's not fair to judge Italian appreciation of terrain by what you see from Italian gardens now. At one time the prospects from the Villa Aldobrandini at Frascati were not the depressing clutter they are today. Every country can point to sylvan retreats engulfed by sprawl. Yet somehow you imagine they mind it less in Italy and spoil larger tracts to less practical end than almost anywhere else.

In this connection, it's interesting to see what happens to an Italian garden and the piece of landscape attached when a non-Italian imagination is put in charge of them. Cetinale near Siena has been in English hands only seventeen years, and the ruling attitude isn't aggressive, but the change is very noticeable. Already the farm buildings seem to blend more and stand out less, which may be only the effect of trimming, planting, and colors of paint, nothing very dramatic.

In the garden there's been a conscious effort to plant in an English way. That's the wrong way to put it, though that's exactly how it looks to someone who's been visiting lots of Italian gardens. No, it's rather that this proprietor wants to grow certain things, and follows the English theory that an interesting garden needs many species, some exotic, surprisingly combined. One consequence of a powerful interest in plants is that their habits of growth often dictate the configurations of the garden. It's as if you built with whatever odd-shaped rocks you found in your fields instead of squaring them to a preimagined standard.

But it's only half the garden at Cetinale where the plants are dictating the spaces in this unheard-of, un-Italian way. From an Italian vantage point the result is exciting near-anarchy, which might ask you to duck under a rose or step round a rosemary jutting into the path.

The main lines at Cetinale are still thoroughly Italian: this garden is based on an alley, very long, very straight, with uneven sides and false closures. Enormous cypresses partly conceal that the ground rises on one side and falls on the other, so that a high wall to the right is matched by a short falling off to the left. On the low side, sheltered by the house, the English garden. On the other, olives terraced into something like formal beds, with a mist of wild flowers rising around their feet.

The old Italian trick of perfect balance where the halves don't match has been subverted in the interest of really English variety. So it isn't the climate which keeps the plant species running in such narrow grooves in Italy, but the architectural obsessions of Italian gardeners.

LLA GUICCIARDINI CORSI SALVIATI, SESTO FIORENTINO

THE PARTERRE

At Gamberaia there's another of these long alleys which dominates the plan, resulting in ungainliness truly inspired. Every bit of this garden, including a large and intractable house, is an appendage of that walk, not necessarily a willing one — some elements try to turn their backs on it, but all are pulled along and given their point in the whole scheme by the alley's insistence. On one side a smallish formal layout terminates in a miniature maze. But the whole formal realm is skewed, off-axis, and the alley remains the center to which you return and from which you are again diverted.

The Italian sense of the meaning of an axis is like no other. At Gamberaia it's the single rule, which, obeyed, gives one an almost complete license to misbehave outside it. Probably the subtlest axis is Villa Lante's. No harm in symmetry, no fear of its stultifying effect, if your three-dimensional imagination is as resourceful as that. And the most dazzling axis is without question the violently steep one at Frascati. It starts from the bottom in a great triangular focus, using three masses of trees and the grass in between to make the eye race toward the villa.

Here the house is, sitting on awkwardly tilted ground, and what does it do? Exaggerates its instability by being tall and wafer-thin. From above, it blocks the view out through converging tree-walls, as though it were a great dam. From below, it towers like a ridiculous giant, still large but rickety when you draw near and see its famished side elevations. And to top everything the roofline makes a single broken pediment, the largest in the world before Philip Johnson, as if the whole villa were nothing but a big doorframe or entrance to the hillside.

This garden is a playground of exaggeration: the grotto right behind the house wears the world's biggest inscription, supported by capitals groaning with the faces of bats and caryatids dwindling to braided dolphin tails. Behind this used to rise a water stair and a series of rougher fountains leading to a streaming rock-face with a cave underneath. Now it is dry, and you stop at each stage to imagine the water's route, racing down the twirly columns and making the tile emblems glitter, say, or running through eyes, nose, and mouth of a stone mask near the top. This is the real water joke nowadays, that there isn't any, which often constitutes a powerful though mournful effect of its own, not as poignant as getting wet, but more lasting.

Occasionally dry fountains are like beggars' cups held out, a silent tale of woe. For a long time now Italian gardens have been acting like places which used to be more extensive, or houses so big all the rooms can no longer be kept in order. Sometimes I wonder if someone doesn't like it that way. Time breaks free and runs unchecked and ever afterwards human effort remains halfhearted.

Apparently it was Rainaldi, not Vignola, who had the obsession with masks that we detect in the upper gardens at Caprarola near Viterbo. There the path has wandered off and up the hillside as if trying to lose itself, until at last you come to one of the most bizarre spaces in any Italian garden. It is a loosely woven double cube of air which sits at the top of one stair and the bottom of another. In the center, a casino people persist in praising, but the great thing is the walls of the outdoor room, formed of twenty-eight herms like the posts of a living fence. They are human individuals formalized into grotesque ornament, but in some way it seems a truer rendition of what it would feel like to turn to stone, truer than something more naturalistic. The grimaces express discomfort at finding that they can't move their legs, that they don't have legs anymore.

Mannerist grotesque always has the potential to degenerate into empty gesture, but it began as a way of bringing buried layers suddenly to light. So it was more not less at home in gardens. The outdoors called forth the beast in man which was released in controlled explosions.

I would like to think the same arguments once raged in these sylvan spots which we are used to hearing on the effects of pornography or televised violence. The subject would have been grottoes and the social damage arising from monstrous grimaces on the faces of garden statues. Had women been assaulted near fountains? Was Bomarzo a cult place among certain criminal elements?

At times extreme artistic forms are bound to go too far. If you really study the masks at Caprarola, which isn't easy with forms camouflaged by moss, you get some very weird ideas. But many visitors must have passed these gruesome displays without really seeing them.

So, should we posit a conspiracy of the grotesque imagination, beaming its products at the susceptible and veiling them from other eyes? It used to be thought that Bomarzo, the most staggering of all Italian boscos, would always be the obscure favorite of a select few. Time and commerce have proved that wrong. Formerly it was authentic nightmare, a desolate patch of overgrowth from which monsters rose, stone animals which threatened to swallow you and careening towers which might bury you. It seemed to take literally or even murderously the promise of violence in Mannerist ornament. A whole landscape had been mined with hatred and resentment until the very air was infected.

Now all that is changed, or so people say. Myself, I am wary of venturing too near the theme park which an aspiring millionaire has made of this landscape I regarded as virtually an obsession of my own. For hundreds of kilometers in both directions billboards lure tourists and their children from the motorway to the new Bomarzo: an actual zoo, some fiberglass dinosaurs, and the bedraggled stone horrors of the sixteenth century. Nothing offends more deeply than serious childishness turned to entertainment for juveniles. It is enough to make one a misanthrope.

The supply of such freakish landscapes is limited in Italy. Oddly enough, another one created by another member of the same Orsini family lies not too far away, near Pitigliano. Formerly one would have said this couldn't be exploited; now who can be sure? Anyway it is at present extremely hard to find. Like Bomarzo it starts with a wild place and turns natural outcroppings into fragments of architecture and sculpture. Most of these occur on the verge of alarming precipices. There are curved benches which appear to be hollowed from sections of enormous columns or from chunks of the architrave of a building bigger than any currently existing. The site has been plundered, and few signs of figure sculpture remain, except for a reclining nude who now resembles a giant wishbone.

Like the other Orsini's, this imagination seems drastically un-Italian. And it was not for two further centuries that a taste for such untended and savage effects caught on at the fringes of the old empire (along the Welsh border, for instance) and then spread tentatively back toward the center.

Many of the names one associates with Italian landscape are foreign ones, like Claude and Poussin. Certain great landscape effects, even Hardian's Villa perhaps, have always been more inspiring to those for whom Italy remains a land of alien wonders. But whoever it inspired first or most, Hadrian's Villa must still be counted one of the great Italian contributions to man's sense of himself as inhabiting most happily, even after all these centuries in civilization, a place poised somewhere between the city and the forest.

No one who studies them only in books can imagine how *humane* some of the great Roman sites have become, so that an influence baleful in origin is softened to something else entirely. The myth is that Hadrian re-created at Tivoli his favorite spots from around the empire, above all Greece and Egypt. To this day, the names of spaces at the villa reflect this theory, which makes the emperor the most infatuated collector who ever was. By now it's hard to check on this because most of the originals have disappeared. If it remembers them at all, Hadrian's garden records vanished wonders, now preserved more fully here than on their home soil.

The doubtful theory has its uses, for this is a landscape in which one is reminded of things, though not perhaps entities or even ways of seeing which Hadrian himself would recognize. Yet his derelict pleasure dome is one of the true sourcebooks of European culture.

An English visitor hears *his* echoes, a French one his. If you are lucky you'll find the wall on which Poussin and Robert Adam, Piranesi and Gavin Hamilton scratched their names. Hadrian's villa is a place intensely hallowed by what it has meant and how it has seemed.

But if it weren't more than that, current visits would be a somewhat barren piety. It remains a truly mythical spot, to which unaccountable rumors cling (that it is closed on Monday, for example, which everyone outside the precincts believes). The villa is the most persuasive instance of the beauty inherent in decay, particularly when applied to man's proudest shaping acts. Here countless pierced and broken vaults resist air and sky less rigidly than they once did. Looking out from these ragged openings, you see buildings through buildings, and further ones beyond, like a receding vista of acts following on one another's heels forever.

It is best in strong sunlight, so that you pass from dark to light and on to further transformations in the series. As gardens exist to do, Hadrian's Villa speaks of death in the gentlest way, saying all these heaped layers couldn't exist without it. Such are the opening hours that anyone who dreams of emulating Hegel's owl and skimming over these ruins at dusk won't have an easy time of it. But if there was ever a landscape which carried its dusk *within,* breeding sadness on the brightest day, this is it. And lest you think this garden really unusual in this regard, wait around in any of them, and it will have you thinking of your end.

After all, what else has the studied neglect met in so many Italian gardens been trying to say?

GIARDINO BUONACCORSI, POTENZA PICENA

ON THE TERRACES

THE GARDENS

TUSCANY

The Boboli Gardens, *Florence*

La Gamberaia, *Settignano*

Palazzo Pfanner, *Lucca;* Villa Mansi, *near Lucca;* Villa Torrigiani, *near Lucca;* Villa Reale, *Marlia*

La Ragnaia, *Castelnuovo Berardenga*

Villa Chigi, *Cetinale, Siena*

BOBOLI

ENTRANCE AT THE PORTA ROMANA

BOBOLI

THE ISOLOTTO

BOBOLI

AT THE FOOT OF THE CYPRESS ALLEY

BOBOLI

AT THE CORNER OF THE ELLIPSE

BOBOLI
——
THE ELLIPSE

BOBOLI

———

THE OLD CITY WALLS

BOBOLI

TOWARD THE PITTI PALACE

BOBOLI

THE KAFFEE HAUS

LA GAMBERAIA

PAINTED WINDOW

LA GAMBERAIA

THE BOSCO

LA GAMBERAIA

BETWEEN THE BOSCO AND THE LEMON GARDEN

LA GAMBERAIA

MAIN AXIS

LA GAMBERAIA

TOPIARY GARDEN

LA GAMBERAIA

TOPIARY GARDEN

PALAZZO PFANNER

FROM THE PALACE STAIRCASE

VILLA MANSI

THE POOL OF DIANA

VILLA TORRIGIANI

GIARDINO SEGRETO

VILLA TORRIGIANI

THE POOL BEHIND THE GIARDINO SEGRETO

VILLA REALE, MARLIA

TOWARD THE GREEN THEATER

VILLA REALE, MARLIA

ANTEROOM OF THE GREEN THEATER

LA RAGNAIA

AT THE CORNER OF THE GARDEN ROOM

48

LA RAGNAIA

ALLEY

VILLA CHIGI

FROM THE FOOT OF THE HILL

VILLA CHIGI

THE VILLA GARDEN

VILLA CHIGI

TOWARD THE HERMITAGE

VILLA CHIGI

TOWARD THE STATUE OF HERCULES

ROME AND VICINITY

Hadrian's Villa, *Tivoli*

Villa Medici, *Rome*

Villa Lante, *Bagnaia*

Villa Farnese, *Caprarola*

Villa Doria Pamphily, *Rome*

Villa Aldobrandini, *Frascati*

HADRIAN'S VILLA

THE CANAL OF CANOPUS

VILLA MEDICI

THE COURTYARD GARDEN AND GIAMBOLOGNA'S MERCURY

VILLA MEDICI

====

THE LOGGIA

VILLA MEDICI

AT THE BASE OF THE OBELISK, COURTYARD GARDEN

VILLA MEDICI

BELVEDERE

VILLA MEDICI

ALLEY FROM THE PINCIO WALL TO THE COURTYARD GARDEN

VILLA MEDICI

NIOBE AND HER CHILDREN

VILLA LANTE

THE PARK

VILLA LANTE

THE UPPER PAVILIONS

VILLA LANTE

ABOVE THE MAIN PAVILIONS

VILLA LANTE

FOUNTAIN, FIRST LEVEL

VILLA LANTE

VIEW TO THE LOWER GARDEN

VILLA LANTE

FOUNTAIN AT ENTRANCE WITH GIAMBOLOGNA'S PEGASUS

VILLA FARNESE

AT THE FOOT OF THE CASINO

VILLA FARNESE

FOUNTAIN AT THE FOOT OF THE CASINO

VILLA FARNESE

THE VIEW OVER THE TOWN

VILLA FARNESE

LOOKING DOWN FROM THE HERM GARDEN

VILLA DORIA PAMPHILY

THE LILY FOUNTAIN

VILLA DORIA PAMPHILY

ENTRANCE OFF THE VIA AURELIA ANTICA

VILLA DORIA PAMPHILY

THE PARK

VILLA DORIA PAMPHILY

THE PARK

VILLA ALDOBRANDINI

THE VILLA, COURTYARD FAÇADE

VILLA ALDOBRANDINI

FAÇADE AND ALLEY

VILLA ALDOBRANDINI

COURTYARD

VILLA ALDOBRANDINI

COURTYARD GARDEN

THE VENETO AND THE MARCHES

Villa Rizzardi, *near Verona*

Villa Pisani, *Stra*

Villa Barbarigo, *Valsanzibio*

Giardino Buonaccorsi, *Potenza Picena*

Villa Brenzone, *Lago di Garda*

VILLA RIZZARDI

ENTRANCE TO GREEN THEATER

VILLA RIZZARDI

LOWER ALLEY

VILLA RIZZARDI

THE VILLA

VILLA RIZZARDI

ENTRANCE TO GREEN THEATER

VILLA RIZZARDI

THE CENTRAL ALLEY

VILLA RIZZARDI

THE BELVEDERE

VILLA RIZZARDI

"RUIN" IN THE BOSCO

VILLA PISANI, STRA

STABLES

VILLA PISANI, STRA

ABOVE THE GARDEN PAVILION

VILLA BARBARIGO

CENTRAL AXIS, WITH ALLEY TO THE VILLA

VILLA BARBARIGO

VIEW UP THE CENTRAL AXIS

VILLA BARBARIGO

THE WATER ENTRANCE

GIARDINO BUONACCORSI

THE TERRACES FROM THE VILLA

GIARDINO BUONACCORSI

THE VILLA AND THE TERRACES

GIARDINO BUONACCORSI

UPPER TERRACE

GIARDINO BUONACCORSI

THE TERRACES

GIARDINO BUONACCORSI

THE TERRACES

GIARDINO BUONACCORSI

THE TERRACES

VILLA BRENZONE

THE MOUNT, WITH ROMAN BUSTS

VILLA BRENZONE

OVER LAGO DI GARDA

THE NORTH

Isola Bella, *Lago Maggiore*

Castello Balduino, *Montalto Pavese*

ISOLA BELLA

THE LAKE

ISOLA BELLA

FROM ABOVE THE THEATER

ISOLA BELLA

THE LAKE

ISOLA BELLA

THEATER AND PARTERRE

CASTELLO BALDUINO

THE TERRACE

CASTELLO BALDUINO

ENTRANCE TO COURTYARD

CASTELLO BALDUINO

ABOVE THE TOPIARY GARDEN

CASTELLO BALDUINO

FROM THE COURTYARD

CASTELLO BALDUINO

THE ORANGERY

CASTELLO BALDUINO

THE TERRACE

CAMPANIA

Palazzo Reale, *Caserta*

CASERTA

THE WATER STAIRCASE

CASERTA

TOWARD THE PALAZZO REALE

CASERTA

TOWARD THE CASCADE

VILLA DORIA PAMPHILY

SELF-PORTRAIT IN PARK

AFTERWORD
BY
GEOFFREY JAMES

A small gray snapshot, taken from behind, shows me or perhaps, judging from the size of the ears, my brother in the Villa d'Este in 1947. The background appears to be the Terrace of 100 Fountains, the most spectacular element of this, the most ostentatious of Late Renaissance gardens. My brother and I chased each other up and down the garden until I slipped on wet moss, leaving a humiliating green patch on the short pants of my flannel suit. Later, like most people who visit Tivoli, we went on to Hadrian's Villa. Here we ran after lizards, trying to tread on their tails, confident that if we ever succeeded, which we never did, they would be able to grow another just as good. From the eighteen months spent in Italy as a child, these are my only real memories: the dampness of the Villa d'Este, the lizards at Hadrian's Villa. It is only with the greatest hesitation that I have revisited either place.

I have often wondered if the vividness of that particular day — a deep body memory that is almost a physical imprint — has led to a photographic enterprise that has preoccupied me for almost a decade. Certainly I am not drawn to Italian gardens by any desire to inhabit them endlessly. For if, as the landscape writer J. B. Jackson has said, the garden is the place we *have* to be, then I would prefer to be in my own modest Canadian retreat, which is on an island the size of Bermuda, and overlooks the Ottawa River. There are a few centenarian oaks, a line of hills behind, and a lawn that slopes down to the river. The garden is unadorned by statues, and the only *giocco d'acqua* is when the power company suddenly lowers the river's water level, transforming the fast, silent current into a series of thunderous standing waves. It is a place in which I can happily be idle, but where I have never had any great urge to photograph. In Italy, by contrast, I can think of only a few gardens where I would care to spend any extended period; but the challenges and complexities of photographing such places seem endless.

I actually began photographing in Italian gardens nearly twenty years ago — a statue here, some topiary there — in the haphazard way people do when they are trying to consume the world with a 35mm camera. I was unaware at the time that there was something that might be called a history of gardens, a discipline that ideally would combine the study of art, architecture, and literature with that of botany and politics and social manners. If I have acquired a little of that knowledge slowly and empirically, I have also taken care to maintain a certain necessary degree of ignorance. A program that is too clearly preordained leads to the entirely uninteresting notion of illustration, which John Szarkowski has succinctly defined as "the application of the techniques of art to make visible a solution that has been reached by other means."

The small camera with which I started out shared one shortcoming with all other conventional cameras. To deal with complex spaces, it requires an extremely wide-angle lens. This in turn causes a violent falling-off in perspective. In 1978, quite by chance, I acquired a 1920s Kodak Panoramic camera which, by the simplest of means, solved this problem. (Teddy Roosevelt also had one, as did the Venetian fabric designer Fortuny.) In this machine, the lens rotates, scanning a curved film plane on an arc of 120 degrees. The negative (which is just short of eleven inches) has a proportion of one to three, prompting some people to ask why the picture is cut off at the top and bottom — the first stage in the realization that all photographs are cuts, the intersection of a rectangle with a cone of light. The Kodak Panoramic is a primitive box whose focusing, shutter speed, and diaphragm are all fixed. But its vices are also its virtues. Because only one picture can be taken at a time, the photographer is obliged to work slowly. Because there are no controls to worry about, the operator can concentrate on the more important decisions in photography: where to stand and when to make the exposure. In some inexplicable way, the camera seems to have something to do with the vision of childhood: spaces appear larger than they really are, and the peripheral is seen with great sharpness. There is, it is true, some distortion, a curving away of planes, but the camera seems at home in the Italian garden, accommodating with ease the ductile forms of the baroque and the multiple points of view created by the designers of these extraordinary places. And while the photographic image has little to do with the way we actually perceive the world, I have an irrational belief that the panorama comes closer to the butterfly-shaped horopter of human vision, more closely duplicating our physical sense of inhabiting space.

When I began working in Italy with this camera in the early 1980s, my guide was Georgina Masson's *Italian Gardens,* a book that combines archival research with an attentive look at the gardens themselves in their twentieth-century form. (The book also has the great merit of overcoming one of the great impediments to learning about Italy, the fact that most knowledge of the country is regionally based and regionally diffused.) Quite early on, I decided that I would let myself be guided by my own intuitions about the quality of each garden — a judgment that is not always based on a garden's capacity to yield satisfying images. In fact, I have found that some of the most important gardens are the most difficult to photograph. The Villa Lante, for instance, one of the most magical places on earth, is as much as anything else a garden of sound. Within the garden proper, it is difficult to escape from the subtle orchestration of falling water — water bubbling down cascades, splashing from fountains, even, when everything is working as it should, dripping from balustrades. There is no easy central passage up and down the Villa Lante, because precedence is always given, quite literally, to the water. And yet, such effects, which are essential to the sense of being in the garden, do not lend themselves to visual representation.

My choice of gardens, then, is largely personal and subjective. Some well-known ensembles, such as the Villa Garzoni at Collodi, seem merely uninteresting — one-dimensional, scenographic spaces consisting of little more than a single prescribed view. Others, like the vast, walled Villa Albani in Rome, belonging to the former royal family, are impenetrable. And at other places, I simply arrived too late. One such garden is Bomarzo, which I first discovered through two memorable but uninformative photographs by the English photographer Bill Brandt, and then through an article by Edmund Wilson, in which he speculated about this dark mockery of Renaissance ideals. The garden was built in the second half of the sixteenth century by an obscure member of the Orsini clan. It was, by all accounts, a strange and original place, a wood converted into a sacred grove, full of monsters and grotesques carved from living rock. On the day I visited Bomarzo in 1984, it had been raining for a week, but that morning there was a warm sun, and the valleys and vineyards on the road from Viterbo were wreathed in vapor. Bomarzo itself, on the spine of a hill, reminded me of a Welsh village — austere, no restaurants, and, one suspected, not a lot of secrets. The garden of the Orsini is in the valley below, invisible from the village, and when I walked down I was overtaken by a succession of large tour buses. At the bottom of the valley there was a parking lot flanked by a large cinder-block building. This was the official entrance that housed a cafeteria, souvenir stands, and video games. The path to the *sacro bosco* went past thatched huts and a sad little zoo. Of the original garden it is hard to tell how much remains. Much of the wood has been replaced by primly planted pines. A red gravel path wends past the monuments, now protected by chicken wire. The buses had disgorged groups of schoolchildren, led by ill-prepared teachers, who read aloud from the official guidebook. Only past the confines of the garden proper, past the graffiti-covered tilted house, where huge, mossy rocks lay in the shade of the ilex, was it possible to sense the pagan spirit of this slightly sinister place.

In the world of painting conservation there comes a moment when, with the oxidization of pigment and the growing evidence of the restorer's hand, a picture may be said to be dead. By this yardstick, Bomarzo, as a living garden, has ceased to exist. We live today in a museum culture, in which the past is simultaneously sanitized and commercially exploited. Perhaps the real metaphor is the zoo. Every time we place an animal in captivity, we change something of its vital nature. What we see is not what we had come to see.

More than any other works of art, gardens are vulnerable to the passage of time, victims not only of the encroachments of nature but of the caprices of fashion and the pressures of speculation. They are susceptible also to being too much used. When the great private Roman estate of the Doria Pamphily family was turned into a public park in 1971, it was engulfed in a wave of systematic vandalism from which it still has not entirely recovered. The problem is not confined to large cities. Even in the pristine countryside around Siena, the spray cans are at work. At the Villa Chigi at Cetinale, the Hermitage that forms the focal point at the end of the garden's main axis was left open and empty for seven years. Not only are its walls covered with the usual violently obscene graffiti, but virtually every piece of masonry has, with a great expenditure of energy, been destroyed. Its English owner speculates that gardens such as his may still be seen as a hated symbol of the powerful autocracy of Italy's past. Certainly for all but a scholarly few, any other symbolic meaning of such gardens has long since disappeared. For while the physical form of the garden persists, the content — the coded classical references of the garden's iconography — is no longer part of any general culture.

The nature of the exercise in which I have been engaged is still not entirely clear to me. In part, these photographs are an act of commemoration and conservation, an attempt to do justice to a subject I consider important. They are also an exploration of the fictive possibilities of the camera, of the peculiar way in which a photograph transforms the world. My only foible — one that requires an excess of patience — has been to picture these places unpeopled. The essentially theatrical nature of Italian gardens has often been remarked upon. But I believe they are best contemplated before the entrance of the actors.

Not long ago, I returned to Tivoli. Miraculously, Hadrian's Villa seemed not to have shrunk at all — it has in fact grown larger with excavation. Like the Boboli gardens in Florence, it appears to absorb an enormous number of visitors without any visible wear and tear. Not so at the Villa d'Este. It was a Sunday and there were probably more than the average 7,000 visitors who go through the garden daily. The vast majority of them were passive consumers of the mass tourism industry, a business that has succeeded in reducing travel to just another form of low-grade distraction. The garden had maintained its tawdry, air-conditioned splendor, but now seemed to have lost any purpose other than to funnel people to the souvenir stands outside. Compared with my childhood memories, the Villa d'Este was diminished, strangely leached of its magic. I could not imagine photographing there, nor even, for that matter, chasing my brother.

BOBOLI, FLORENCE

THE ISOLOTTO

NOTES ON THE GARDENS

❧ *The Boboli Gardens*

One of the most marvelous public parks in the world, the Boboli began as a display ground for Medici power at the back of a magnificent urban villa. Many of the leading Mannerist architects and designers had a hand in its complex development over the last half of the sixteenth and first half of the seventeenth centuries.

The original axis leaves the palace and climbs the slope behind until it reaches the old city walls. Along the way are pools often used for elaborate naumachiae (such as the siege of a Turkish castle by eighteen Christian ships in 1589), a complicated grotto, and the vast amphitheater where cumbrous pageants were staged. These features are likely to strike modern sensibility as inert relics of outworn taste. Geoffrey James gravitates to the fringes, the cross axis, and the Isolotto at the furthest extremity from the palace.

To either side of the cross axis were formerly found traps for songbirds, a zoo, and a botanical garden. Now this part has an overgrown and mazelike character.

Like the amphitheater, the Isolotto is modelled on ancient Roman precedent. It dates from 1618 and remains one of the most entrancing marriages of ultraformality and unpredictable movement. Essentially it is a stone island overloaded with sculpture and linked to the mainland by bridges lined with lemon trees. The water teems with goldfish and the elliptical geometry is endlessly diverting.

❧ *La Gamberaia*

This is justly regarded as one of the best Tuscan gardens. It is particularly astonishing for what it fits into small compass, and for the oddity of its proportions, which could occur nowhere but in Italy.

La Gamberaia is organized along a wide grass axis of delightful concavity (see page 39). On one side the villa, a water parterre and breathtaking views of Florence. On the other, a bosco hiding behind a wall or elevated on a platform (see page 37). Next to it lies an ingenious grotto-garden which insidiously deepens, then a limonaia, then another bosco. After this the grass avenue crosses the road and ends in a melodramatic cul-de-sac. Along the whole back edge a novel relation is formed with the surrounding agrarian landscape.

Though there has been a garden here since the sixteenth century, the main lines as we have them date from the eighteenth. It suffered badly from bombing in the last war and has been carefully reconstructed since.

❧ *Palazzo Pfanner*

An eighteenth-century garden attached to a grandiose Lucchese palace of the seventeenth century. The trees visible at the back of the picture line the Renaissance ramparts of the city, from which good views of this inaccessible garden are obtained.

Pfanner is most remarkable because it lies within the walls, probably the largest old garden to survive more or less intact in Lucca.

❧ *Villa Mansi*

A tantalizing place, where little of the old layout survives. Filippo Juvara worked here in the eighteenth century. His, perhaps, is the bold Baroque pool in the picture. Around it, vast tracts in the English taste.

❧ *Villa Torrigiani*

There is an irony in the name of this garden, for it was the new Torrigiani owners who swept seventeenth-century planting aside to redo their grounds in English style in the nineteenth century.

Two sections survived, represented in the pictures, a sunken *giardino segreto* and a pool above it.

Formerly this haven could be operated like a trap. Guests would be imprisoned in the secret garden by a wall of water at the entrance, and then chased down the paths by sprays which erupted in sequence among the pebbles.

❧ *Villa Reale*

One of the great charms of this vast place is the dishevelment of its outlying parts. In fact it is another seventeenth-century domain partially anglicized in the nineteenth century, this time by Napoleon's sister.

After wandering through seas of high grass which lap the edges of weed-choked lakes, after passing dilapidated chapels and lava-bedizened grottoes, the visitor comes to a choice sequence of pools, gates, and fountains, culminating in the little green theater. This is a splendidly useless space with box hedges for seats and terra-cotta actors clogging the stage. The photographs show the various preludes to this experience.

❧ *La Ragnaia*

Every Tuscan garden from the sixteenth century was likely to include a *ragnaia,* or netting place. These were small groves of low trees into which songbirds would be lured, then captured in nets, and finally served up at table.

The Ragnaia at Castelnuovo Berardenga is an extremely precious survival. Here the trap takes the ornamental form of a parterre — four rooms of trees are connected by alleys which appear to be excavated from the solid vegetable medium which lies round about.

By now these ancient ilex have grown much too large to throw nets over, and they produce a gloom which must be far from the original effect.

❧ *Villa Chigi*

Laid out by Carlo Fontana for the nephew of a pope, Cardinal Chigi, who is reputed to have arranged the murder of a fellow cardinal and built some penitential features into this garden to make up for it.

These include a steep rustic stair to a hermitage and various hermits' resting places in a wood called *Thebaid* after the bit of the Egyptian desert favored by early Christian ascetics. It must be said that this is not a convincingly morbid or penitential place. Hercules marks the terminus of the axis in one direction; the strange chapel like an oversized dovecote marks it in the other.

Once again, various features are laid out along this thoroughfare, which is seen in pages 50 and 3 (looking toward the villa), 52 (toward the hermitage), and 53 (toward Hercules). Now English-style planting quietly subverts the grand order on one side, and terraced olives fill the other (see page 15).

✤ *Hadrian's Villa*

The myth is well known that this learned emperor wanted to remind himself of his travels through the empire by reproducing foreign sights on the grounds of his villa at Tivoli.

Later gardens have certainly been inspired by his: the Isolotto at the Boboli derives from Hadrian's so-called Marine Theater (a fantastic name coined by Pyrro Ligorio, designer of the Villa d'Este).

The Canopus canal (see page 55) was the setting for elaborate entertainments. The apse form at the far end held a large dining room.

✤ *Villa Medici*

A lone survivor among the sixteenth-century gardens of great Roman villas.

It occupies the site of a famous classical garden and has inspired not only the many French artists who have lived there since it became the seat of the French Academy in 1803, but such visitors as Velázquez, who portrayed it in two famous oil sketches.

Giambologna's Mercury, one of the most reproduced garden statues in the world, presides over the courtyard while one of the Villa Medici's enclosed garden rooms houses Niobe and her children, a surrealistic grouping of figures excavated from Hadrian's Villa. From the bosco, incongruously, one gets wonderful views of Rome (see page 59), for this is after all the ultimate hilltop garden.

✤ *Villa Lante*

In some sense the finest of all Italian gardens, for the essentially architectural imagination which fuses its diverse elements in a single symphonic composition. It is the subtlest of all gardens on slopes. The slope is gentler and the articulation more complex than in its nearest rivals, at Caprarola and Frascati.

Vignola is generally credited with the design, working for the erudite Cardinal Gambara, who was censored for the expense by the pope and had to divert funds intended for the second pavilion to a hospital instead.

The second pavilion is of course one of the inspired strokes of the design, built after all, though eleven years late. It is relatively modest in scale, but practically speaking superfluous, a sign of the maker's conceptual ardor.

Geoffrey James' photographs generally forsake the more intricate lower parts for the obscure reaches behind and above the pavilions, deep in shade and coursed through by unquiet water, which only comes dependably to rest in the open and at the bottom.

❧ Villa Farnese

The construction of this garden overlaps that of Villa Lante. It was begun by Vignola in the mid-sixteenth century and finished by Rainaldi almost fifty years later.

These gardens make a strange addendum to one of the most magnificent and forbidding of Renaissance palaces. The building began as a fortress, designed by Sangallo and Peruzzi, and it has never outgrown this rugged origin.

All but one of the photographs were taken in the more interesting part of the garden, which lies at a considerable distance from the palace, high on the slope behind it. After a woodland walk comes a pair of grottoes divided by a stair, down the middle of which water runs in a raised course. At the top is an elephantine fountain and around the little garden behind is a series of herms carved by Bernini's father, Pietro. This is Mannerism at its most personable.

❧ Villa Doria Pamphily

As it exists today, the Doria Pamphily is not one thing. At its core lies Algardi's pavilion, stuck all over with antique fragments, and his *giardino segreto* beneath it. These are practically the only seventeenth-century features in near enough their original form to work as intended. Much nineteenth-century interference obscures the pools and fountains nearby. Among other delights there is a grotesque pseudo-Romanesque funerary chapel.

But the great glory of the place is the park, with its famous umbrella pines. It was a favorite with painters of the last century, and it absorbs today's crowds of joggers with ease.

The intention of the designers may have been to achieve English results, but some of these species are intrinsically and unalterably formal in their effect.

❧ Villa Aldobrandini

This archetypal Baroque garden was built in a short period (1598–1603) by Giacomo della Porta and Carlo Maderna.

Quite unusually, the villa, a summer retreat, is here worthy of its place in the garden. In essence it is a great pediment, rearing up very majestically, but only two rooms thick. Immediately behind it is the water theater (see page 78), formerly full of water jokes and automata but now entirely still and dry. Even the water stair on the wild slope behind the villa has subsided to a large damp spot. Page 79 shows one of the quiet quincunxes symmetrically disposed on either side of the central axis at the level of the villa-platform.

❧ Villa Rizzardi

This has claims to be considered the last true Italian garden, designed in the closing years of the eighteenth century by Luigi Trezza.

It consists of three ample promenades at different levels, from which there are many sweeping views of the surrounding country. In the middle is one of the most famous of garden theaters, with a huge flat semicircle in front of the seats. At the top level, the bosco with its charming ruin, and finally the belvedere, a lovely example of the type.

ℭ *Villa Pisani*

This villa of daunting scale comes equipped with a garden in the French taste, designed slightly earlier in the eighteenth century. It was the project of Alvise Pisani, who had been Venetian ambassador in Paris.

There is a large maze with a wonderful viewing tower at the center. This idea is realized again, in more diffuse form, by the feature seen on page 89. This hexagonal arch, with twisting elevated walkways along which statues bob, commands views down all the alleys radiating from this central point. It is a peculiarly Italian fantasy of power.

ℭ *Villa Barbarigo*

There are rumors that formerly you could enter this garden by boat. Or at least, that following the system of canals which connected it to Venice you would pull up at the water gate (page 92) and disembark.

Formerly it was famous for rare plants, but now it is pleasantly overgrown. Only the rabbit island and a few pools and fountains survive to remind one of its former elaboration.

ℭ *Giardino Buonaccorsi*

One of the least known and most magical of all Italian gardens. It inhabits an out-of-the-way place, far from major centers of culture.

It remains virtually undocumented and, unlike the other great gardens, is not connected with the name of a famous designer. Writers usually assume it dates from the eighteenth century, but if this is so, much of the detail in upper parterres is curiously retarded.

The Buonaccorsi contains the most delightful garden statues in the world. There is a great wealth of them, disposed on a succession of five narrow terraces which decline gently down a slope. The population is denser at the top, but some of the best surprises are saved for last. As the pictures show, the cast includes emperors, mythical and allegorical figures, tramps, beggars, dwarves and rustics of all kinds.

ℭ *Villa Brenzone*

Here in a wonderful position overlooking Lago di Garda remnants survive of a garden created in the sixteenth century for a philosopher-lawyer who wrote a treatise on the solitary life and allowed the public access to his preserve.

The circle of emperors' busts (page 98) decorates a little artificial mount surrounded by old cypresses.

ℭ *Isola Bella*

This garden fills most of an island in Lago Maggiore. It took forty years to build and represents a considerable feat of engineering, which has drawn awed praise in the years since it was completed (around 1670). Incidentally, the accompanying villa is only now being completed.

It consists of ten terraces hewn from rock and founded on grottoes, which are some of the most enchanting in existence.

The crown of the whole experience is the water theater (pages 102, 104), where one finds tier on tier of statued niches topped by a fringe of putti.

ℭ *Castello Balduino*

An eighteenth-century garden which had fallen into such decay by the beginning of this century that its scholarly reconstruction probably required some inventive skill.

The outstanding features here are two, an upper terrace and a lower topiary plot, probably the most famous in Italy. Many Italian gardens *began* with superb views which have been spoiled by recent suburban sprawl and the like. At Castello Balduino the prospect remains much as it always was, and this bit of luck means that it is now the most beautifully situated garden in Italy.

ℭ *Palazzo Reale*

This is the Italian super-Versailles, built north of Naples for the Bourbon king by Vanvitelli in 1752–74.

Its great feature is an axis leading from the palace (a rectangle 247 by 184 meters) straight to the cascade of Diana about 3 kilometers distant. Every lover of gardens should probably cover this stupefying course once in his or her life.

LIST OF PLATES

Numbers preceding each entry refer to page numbers

ACKNOWLEDGMENTS

My first debt of gratitude is to those who are, in the broadest sense of the term, caretakers of these places. This group includes owners, state officials, and, of course, the gardeners and caretakers themselves. Over the past decade, I have been shown much kindness and consideration by all three groups. In particular I should like to thank Prince Aldobrandini, Signor Fabio Pizzoni Ardemani, Balthus and his successor at the Villa Medici in Rome, Msr. Jean-Marie Drot, Count Guarienti di Brenzone, Miguel Berrocal, Lord Lambton, Signora Alessandra Marchi Pandolfini and her late father-in-law Signor Marchi, Countess Cristina Guerrieri Rizzardi, Signor Salom, and Signor Perugini and his fellow-owners of the Giardino Buonaccorsi. I am also grateful to Dr. Litta Medri, curator of the Boboli Gardens, Signor A. D'Offrizio of Hadrian's Villa and the Soprintendenze per i Beni Ambientali e Architettonici of Rome, Florence, and the Veneto. In my pursuit of gardens, I have profited from the advice of Ippolito Pizzetti and the late Isa Belli Barsali. Invaluable logistic support has come from my friends Gilbert Reid and Elena Solari of the Canadian Cultural Centre in Rome, and from Pat Weaver of the American Academy in Rome. For the opportunity of presenting this work in published form, I should like to thank Mark Greenberg of Abrams for his initial support of the project, and my editor, Ruth Peltason, for her diligence and sensitivity. Carol Robson, the designer, has shown great care and consideration for the images. Finally, none of this work would have been possible had not my wife, Jessica, shared my deeply nomadic instincts, and been willing to uproot our family from time to time.

At various critical junctures in my life, I have received support from the Canada Council, the Graham Foundation for Advanced Studies in the Fine Arts, and the John Simon Guggenheim Memorial Foundation. For the periods of grace and freedom they have provided these enlightened bodies cannot be thanked too much.

G.J.